GR

A Centering Corporation Resource
By Joy and Dr. Marvin Johnson

from the original title by
Ed Vining

The beautiful poems in this book are by
Jean McGrew.
They are copyrighted by the author
and used here with loving permission.

ISBN# 1-56123-085-5
SAN:298-1815

Centering Corporation
1531 N Saddle Creek Rd
Omaha NE 68104
Phone: 402-553-1200   Fax: 402-553-0507

When you grieve -

you're like a tree hit by a tornado.
Some of your roots are pulled up.
You're twisted and bent.

Your leaves have been stripped.
Your bark is loosened.
And worst of all,
one of your big limbs has been brutally
broken off.
You will never be the same.

Eventually, slowly, your roots grow back.
You experience a new growth of leaves.
You straighten up and reach out again.

But the limb never grows back.
It becomes covered with a natural scar tissue.

For ever after, you will be aware of the tornado
and the tremendous change it made
in your life.

We hope we can stand with you in the storm,
that we can be there as you weather this grief and
as you look forward to standing tall once more.

Joy Johnson
Dr. Marvin Johnson

Grief Seasons

In wintertime
the grieving tree
is cold
numb
naked.

When springtime comes
the grieving tree
seems warmer
softer
gentler.

In summertime
the grieving tree
feels hot
full
stifled.

When autumn comes
the grieving tree
begins to
let go. . .

Jean McGrew

Grief affects every aspect of your being.
You will have changes occurring simultaneously —
emotionally, behaviorally, physically,
cognitively and spiritually.
*from **More Than Surviving***

It kept running through my head:
'Humpty Dumpty sat on a wall.
Humpty Dumpty had a great fall.
All the king's horses and all the king's men
couldn't put Humpty Dumpty together again.'
Now my husband was gone, and no one could ever put him
or me together again.

Grief is the emotional reaction to loss
Mourning is the expression of that grief.

When someone you love dies, you feel like Humpty
Dumpty. You can compare yourself to eggs as well as trees.
You're scrambled, you feel cracked, you feel raw and then
you get hard-boiled. But, as one member of a bereavement
support group said, *Someday we'll be sunny side up again.*

Grief takes time.
You won't get over it in a month or even a year.
In fact, you never get over it.
You never get through it.
You blend it into your life and make it part of you.

Basically, you go through shock, despair and finally,
you reach recovery. There are days when you concentrate
on making it through the next 10 minutes, and days you
feel pretty good. You will adjust your life and find a "new
normal," and that means going through that first year and
facing those important days:
anniversaries
Christmas\Hannakuh
birthdays
special days, important only to you.

The day that really got to me was the first day of hunt-
ing season. He always looked forward to that day, always
had plans. I took his hunting boots, sat down with them
and cried all morning.

When the second year comes around you can say, "I got
through it last year, I can do it again."

Feelings

Tears are a river that takes us somewhere.
We don't remember who said those words, but they're important. This is a time to cry and cry and cry; to rage and pound pillows. This is a time to come to terms with what has happened; to acknowledge your loss.

Disbelief — it's hard to believe the death happened. Even if you knew the death was coming, you are not ready. The phone rings and you know it's her. You catch a glimpse of him on a crowded street, and at the playground, there she is again. It's as if you are searching for your person.

I'd open the garage door and think, 'Oh, good! Charlie's home early,' then I'd remember that it was just his car. Charlie wasn't here anymore.

It's common and normal to begin to talk to the one who died. Sometimes you just forget he's not standing there beside you. At other times, you speak purposefully and directly to your person. We encourage talking out loud to your loved one.
Tell her what you feel.
Tell him what's happening.
Say the things you left unsaid.
Obviously, it's wise to do this when you're alone, but if you don't and someone catches you mumbling to yourself, just say it's good to have a conversation with an intelligent person now and then.

Facing the reality of death is very hard.

A few weeks after my mother's funeral I called the house, knowing full well my father would be at work. I let it ring 17 times. Seventeen! My mother did not answer. I hung up the phone, slid to the floor and cried for hours.
                                    *from **Dancing With The Skeleton***

Sorrow — you can't lose anyone or anything of value without being sad.

Pat Page, in his book, *Cowbells and Courage* says, "Go ahead and baby yourself all you want. Men do too cry, and they should. That crap about men not crying is poppycock. Cry as often as you need and don't worry about making a fool of yourself in front of other people. Who has a better reason to cry? Laughing and crying are excellent therapy, but keep in mind, your world has *not* come to an end. You have lost a lot, but you also have a lot left."

You may be afraid that you'll start crying and not be able to stop. You'll stop. When your body is tired enough and your emotions are played out, the tears will stop.

It may seem as if you'll never be happy again. You may go to a bereavement support group and hear people laugh. You may wonder how anyone can laugh when you're hurting so badly, but somewhere, way back in your head there's a little voice calling your name. It's saying, "You'll laugh again sometime, too."

You were so happy, said my mother.
You'll be happy again, said my sister.
I can't wait to see you happy again, said Aunt Faygie.
Happy? Oh yes, happy...
Well, I do recall a few bits and pieces of happy.
Like in happy birthday, right?
And Happy Hanukkah, Happy New Year
And I'm soooo Happy.
Yes, I remember Happy.
It was, if I recall, a sort of lilt-y feeling.
It was awhile ago, but yes, I remember.
Our favorite salad bar, couch cushions,
Free trolly to the Gallery.
Yes, yes. Sometime, someplace, in some language,
there IS a happy.
Yes, Ma, I remember happy well.
Yes, Rozzy, I will be happy again.
And Faygie, especially Faygie,
I, also, can't wait.
from She Was Born: She Died

If only . . .
    If only . . .
        If only . . .
    Guilt! Guilt! Guilt!

I said if only I had insisted he go to the doctor sooner, and if only I'd said what I needed to say. I went on and on until finally I got to where I was thinking, 'if only I'd never married him in the first place I wouldn't hurt like this.'

Kelly Osmont, in her book, *More Than Surviving* points out the difference between guilt and regret.

Guilt is when we purposely commit a hurtful act.

Regret is when we realize we could have done something different.

Exploring your regrets is healthy and normal. You can learn from them. If there were things you left unsaid to the person who died, write them down, make them into a letter to that person. The learning comes when we no longer leave things unsaid, when we tell our children and our spouses and others that we love them; when we let the wisdom of our regrets guide us in our future and present relationships.

If you could have prevented your person's death, you would have. If you could have known everything and made things easier, you would have. Ed Ames in his book, *A Look In The Mirror* says,

"The morning before Merideth died, I left her alone to go for a long bike ride. If I had not gone, her heart would have stopped anyway. I know I should not feel guilt about it. But I did. *If only I had known she had so few hours left, I would have....* Would have what? Spent the time with her, I assume. But who could assure me that would have made her death better or easier for either of us? Useless questions, without answers, they nevertheless bothered me. "

Depression

We cannot lose anyone we love or anything of value without feeling depressed. Even when you weren't grieving, there were days when you were down. Now they seem more intense, more frequent. They feel like a dark cloud enveloping you from head to toe.

I honestly would stay in bed all day, curl up and never open my eyes if I didn't have to eventually get up and go to the bathroom.

Depression is a normal part of grief. We're a society that so fights depression that you have to be careful. It's easy to go to a doctor or a counselor, say you're depressed and have them hand you an antidepressant. True, if you're really dysfunctional, you may need something. But be sure whoever is handing them out knows you are **grieving.**

Wise is the person who stays away from drugs and alcohol. These merely squash your grief and it will rise up later. Believe us, grief will have its way with you. It's best to lean into it, feel it, go with it, accept it as a part of you right now.

Fears

Death holds up a magnifying glass and shows us how fragile life is. You may be frightened of a lot of things now. Every time someone gets a cold, you shiver. Every time someone you love starts on a long trip, you worry. Every time another paper is put in front of you and you're told to sign it you hesitate.

Two things may help with fears:
List your fears on one side of a sheet of paper.
On the other side, put down what you can do about each.

And most importantly — talk about them. Find someone who will listen without telling you how you *should* feel or do and share your feelings and fears.

Anger

Pat Page's wife had been sick a long time. She kept a cowbell by her bed to call him. He listened so intently for it that when the neighbor's windchimes blew in the night he jumped out of bed. The first thing he did after her body was taken from the house, was grab the cowbell, take it outside, put it on a stump and smash it. Anger is a part of grief.

I sat in the emergency room. I knew he was dead. His motorcycle had smashed into a pole. Finally, I couldn't take it any longer. I hit the wall with my fist and yelled, 'I hate motorcycles!'

You may be angry at doctors, others involved, yourself. You may be angry at the person who died. You may be angry at God.

We think it's all right to be angry at God. The prophets of the old testament threw some strong words toward Heaven. The prayers of anger are real prayers. They come from the gut as well as the heart. If you do get angry at God, remember — God can take it.

One widow bought an empty garbage can just so she could throw in the dishes she'd bought at a second-hand store expressly for that purpose. She needed to heave something, to hear it break. She felt better.

If you're a runner, running can help release anger, as will any exercise. You can take a kitchen towel, fold it double and beat on your mattress. You can write your anger down and you can talk it out, too.

I was mad at everyone. She had killed herself...completed suicide they called it in a kindly way. One day I went to her grave, sat and talked to her, yelled a little and said, 'I'm so mad, Lynne, I could kill you!' Then I heard what I said and I laughed. It was a release for me.

The Crazies

You simply feel you're losing it.
You worry about going out of your mind.
You stand in the grocery store and stare for 15 minutes
    trying to choose between the peas and the carrots.
You forget things.
You lose track of time.
You feel spacey.
You feel numb.
You're overwhelmed by simple chores.
You think you're going crazy.

This is a crazy time. It doesn't make sense. You do things you would never do if you weren't grieving.

Ed Ames tells another story in *A Look In The Mirror*. This concerns a high school principal whom everyone said was taking his wife's death very well. "I found myself outside my house, striding along the street shouting out her name. *Marion! Where are you? Marion! Marion! Where are you?* Fortunately, a neighbor came out, took me by an arm and invited me in for a cup of tea. Until he took hold of me, I had no awareness of what I was doing, or where I was! The experience was deeply unsettling."

Deeply unsettling.
Very accurate words.

At this time, when you find yourself in mountains of paper work, cards to write, calls to answer, decisions to make, your mind takes a vacation.

This is one of the most frustrating parts of grief because you feel as if you're losing control. It may help if you:
Make lists.
Keep notes and reminders in a file that stays in one place.
Have someone you trust double-check with you about
    appointments and important meetings.
Recognize that even though it seems strange at times, these feelings are all normal.

Frustrating Things

"Deeply unsettling "could also describe some of the experiences you face in settling the estate, filing insurance claims, deciding what to do with belongings.

I was so angry with both my lawyer and my insurance man that one day I decided to stop pacing and called them both. I told them that I was the consumer. I was hiring them not the other way around and I expected them to do their jobs and to keep me informed.

There are many good attorneys and insurance representatives. These are the ones who will remind you that indeed, you are the boss. Tell them what you want. Ask them what you need to do.

"ASK! ASK! ASK! Ask what the steps are, what **you** must do, what your lawyer will do. Knowing clearly what is expected of you will keep your mind more at ease and very likely speed the process as well." Ed Ames.

Be prepared to wait. These things take time and that isn't all bad. Time helps you clear your head. Take a tape recorder or a friend with you so you have a record of what is said. Take notes. Your mind is fuzzy anyway, so recording things or writing them down makes sense.

Our bereavement support group is called, **The Bereavement Support Group**, but members privately call it the BS Group because of what you have to put up with when someone dies.

There will be times when you feel defeated, when you think not one more bad thing can happen to you. When you feel that way, start writing. Call someone and talk it out. And if at all possible, find a bereavement support group in your area. They provide a safe place to talk and everyone there really does understand how you feel. They feel the same way, too. At the very least, try it for one, or better yet, two sessions. You don't have to talk, just listen.

Precious Things

Clear out belongings when **you** are ready. If family come from a distance for the funeral, it's fair to ask them what they want and give them what they can carry home and what you're ready to give. Again, don't rush. Keep what you need and want.

When Gracie Allen died her husband, George Burns, got great comfort from sleeping in her bed. Arranging a few of your loved one's precious things near your bed may be comforting, too.

Many widows wear their husband's sweaters and shirts. One daughter proudly wore her father's tailored coat. She was 80 years old. He had died when she was 60. Kids use Mommy's T-shirts for sleep shirts after she's gone. One young granddaughter claimed her grandpa's stetson because he had taught her to ride horses.

Clearing things out will bring tears, and while they may be uncomfortable for awhile, they're healing tears. The memories come back.

Wallet
Folded leather
with plastic pieces
of your Earth self
peeking
from each
pocket:
brief
poignant
statements
of who
you were
but are no more...

(You expired
before they did.)

Jean McGrew

All The Other People

It seems strange. Someone you love has died and the world goes on. People shop. They go to work. They laugh. And you are, as one widow said, experiencing *the winter of frozen dreams.*

I'm so sorry, they say.
How are you? they say.
I'm fine. I say.
Just fine.

When you're grieving, Fine *is a four-letter word!*

Darcie Sims, author and lecturer, says when you grieve you carry a smile-on-a-stick. When someone asks how you are, you just hold up your smile on a stick and say, *Fine.*

While you are hurting on the inside, you feel forced to smile on the outside. Remember, this is a time to take care of yourself. You don't have to take care of everyone else. If other people are upset or bothered by your tears, that's their problem, not yours. You don't break down when you cry; it's more like a gentle melting. It's all right to gently melt now and then in public.

Ed Ames writes: "*But if I'm in a public place, I'll feel conspicuous,* you say. Probably. So what *can* you do if someone sees you crying, or hears you, and asks what the problem is? How do you handle that? The best advice I had was from a realtor in South Carolina: *Simply say you were just reminded of a precious or cherished moment, and, 'It caught me unaware. I'll be fine in a moment or two.'* That struck me as sensible, straight-forward advice. It certainly would have helped me."

You are bound to meet people who do not know of the death. Simply tell them straight out. Talk about it. If they lean toward you and are interested, talk more. If they act as if they've just spotted an eight-foot lizard and need to get away, forget it. Find someone else to talk to.

Framing

Talking is probably the single most important thing you can do to help yourself and take care of yourself. We call talking about your person's death, how you feel, what has happened "framing."

Someone said, *Anything can be borne if a story can be told.* Telling your story is healing.

As you tell what happened and how you felt over and
  over you'll notice some changes:
Your story gets briefer, more concise.
You begin to highlight the main details.
Your feelings become clearer, easier to handle.
Meaning slowly, gently begins to surface.

It's as if you've made a picture of your story. All the paragraphs are in place. The commas are where they should be. There's a beginning, a middle, an end.

Finally, after you've told it enough, you can hang your story on the wall. It's framed with your tears. It can stay on the wall of your life and you can look at it whenever you want. You can take it down and handle it, show it to other people. The important thing is, you'll always have it, but you don't have to carry it around with you all the time.

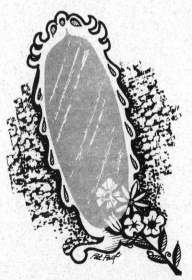

Listen To The Children

Small children have a limited concept of death. They may ask questions over and over again. They may play and act as if nothing has happened or the slightest thing may set them off screaming with rage.

She was so afraid. She clung to me and I held her and hugged her until she was ready to get down and play.

Like you, they may have difficulty eating and sleeping. Aches and pains and stomach upsets may occur. Fears, guilts, feelings and younger behavior is normal.

Children over 6 are beginning to understand about death. They will have many questions. Fear that death will come to them or someone else they love is common. Their emotions, like yours, will go up and down.

After age 10, they know what death is. They may act like grown-ups at times and younger than their age at others.

No matter what the child's age, you can help:
Be honest. The truth is easier to digest than fantasy.
Answer their questions as best you can.
Talk about the person who died. Invite them to talk.
Share your feelings. Crying is all right and helpful.
Look at old pictures, letters and home videos with them.

Let them take part in the funeral and saying goodbye if they want to do so. Children can draw pictures and write letters to put in the casket to be buried with their person. They can ask questions of the funeral director and if possible, have their own time to say goodbye. An excellent little book, *Thank You For Coming To Say Goodbye* gives an example of an actual funeral home orientation for children when someone dies.

Give the children you love time, space, and a lot of hugs. They need to know that no matter what, they'll be cared for and loved.

Grieving Teens

Your teenagers are likely to have their own style of grieving. They may become angry at you, friends, the world. They may withdraw into their music or want to be only with their friends. Problems with drugs, alcohol and school performance may surface. On the other hand, they could turn out to be your best support at this painful time.

Teens will grieve in their own way and in their own time. Accept the differences in each person's grieving style.

Teens need to feel comfortable with all their feelings.
Let them know you will be expressing your feelings.
Let them know it is all right to express theirs, too.
Let them know you are there to talk when they are ready.
Let them know it is okay to cry and be angry.
Most of all, let them know you love them.

Remember together. Bring out old pictures and share memories. Help each other. If your young person is interested in a support group, find one for them. It's healing to be able to share their feelings and loss with others.

Ideas for teens:
Write a letter to the person who died.
Keep an ongoing letter about feelings and changes.
Draw or write poetry.
Keep a journal.
Make a scrapbook of memories and photos.
Plant a tree. Water and care for it.
Light a candle in honor of your person.
Create a family ritual to remember your loved one.
Have a dinner in honor of your loved one and
serve his or her favorite foods.

So it wasn't the normal thing to have spaghetti for Christmas dinner, but we did it in honor of my Dad. It was his favorite food. We hung up his stocking and put fresh flowers in it. Best of all, we remembered him and laughed. The day wasn't as hard as I thought it would be.

Saying Goodbye

Ed Vining, a caring funeral director who first wrote the book by this title speaks of the funeral:

> The visitation is the social release
> of the body.
> The funeral is the spiritual release
> of the body.
> The burial is the physical release
> of the body.

"The first funeral I attended was that of a 24-year-old friend. We went to a small town in northern Iowa, to a small country church. I grabbed a friend's hand and walked to the front of the church where an open casket sat. I thought how strange he looked. How thin his cancer had made him.

After the service, we followed the casket into the grave-yard beside the church. The churchbell tolled 24 times as his friends carried him to his grave. It was February and the wind and snow were blowing like hardened tears in our faces. Then the pastor announced that everyone was invited inside for lunch.

How awful! I thought. *This is a very serious and solemn time. How could anyone have lunch after this?* But I was hungry. I went back into the church to a kitchen filled with the smell of warm soup and hot sandwiches.

Everyone was quiet for awhile, then someone laughed. Soon the room was filled with conversation, hugs for the family, movement again. Life after death. In one startling moment I saw the wisdom of my elders and other cultures in making a celebration a part of grief."

Joy Johnson

Funerals and memorial services are for the living.

If you are reading this before planning your service, keep in mind that you have a lot of options. You can bring pictures of your person to put around the room where the service will be held. You can select special music and objects.

When my mother died, her quilt collection and her napkin collection were on display. At the end of the service her grandchildren handed a carnation to everyone who came. I only wish I had thought to get a tape with harmonica music on it. She played a really mean mouth harp and loved that bouncy rhythm.

You can dress the person's body in clothes you select.

He was buried in his jeans and his flannel shirt — what he had worn every day. All the ranchers brought their branding irons, held them over the fire and burned their brand into his wooden coffin. His father made that coffin.

You can design the service.

We all shared memories of Pat. Sure we cried a lot, but who cares? I told about getting lost hunting mushrooms with her. Someone else told about how a permanent frizzed her hair. All the while her favorite music played softly.

You can help prepare the body if you like. If you are of Jewish or Native American faiths, you already have a culture which helps you do this. No matter what your nationality or religion, you can ask to do something. Parents have bathed and dressed their babies. Mothers have braided their daughter's hair and daughters have caringly and lovingly put their mother's favorite makeup on her face.

We brought her eye shadow and blush. We put her foundation on her and she looked good. Then my sister said, 'Something's wrong.' We realized the funeral director had put on very conservative earrings and our mom was not conservative! We returned with her big brass dangling ones.

Whether or not the funeral is over, there are many things you can do to say goodbye.

♦ Arrange for a family memorial service on your person's birthday or death anniversary.

♦ Keep a journal for at least a year. At the end of the year look back and see how much better you feel now. Dedicate the last page of the journal to your loved one.

♦ Make a remembrance tree. Directions are in the back of this booklet.

♦ Write a letter to your person. Say everything you need to say. Then write a letter back from your person to you.

♦ Light a special candle each day and whisper *goodbye.*

♦ Make a photo album of your loved one.

♦ Plant a tree or flower bed.

♦ Donate to your favorite charity or organization in your person's memory.

I heard of a widow who every year, on her husband's birthday, went to the store and bought a complete man's outfit in her husband's size. Then she gave it to a local shelter. I really liked that idea, so I did it, too.

♦ Talk to the person who died. Find a quiet place, say everything you need to say. Cry as much as you need to cry.

I felt so guilty! I sat at my table with a cup of coffee and said, 'Marilyn, it was my fault! The accident was all my fault!' I sobbed and sobbed. Then I pictured her in my mind. All I saw was her gentle smile and her hand reaching out as if she wanted to touch me. I felt forgiven by her and forgiven by myself, too.

♦ Go to the cemetery. Take flowers, or a toy or any object that can be left there. Sit beside the grave and do whatever goodbye feels right for you.

The most beautiful deer stepped out of the woods by the cemetery. I had just finished saying goodbye and it was a very special sign for me.

Taking Care of Yourself

I never raised my voice when he was alive. He did everything, took care of everything. But today I called my insurance man and said, 'This is mine! I need the money and I need it now!' It wasn't like me at all.

What's important is that you take care of yourself.

But I don't know how to do that now!

You just did.

Taking care of yourself means:

♦Speaking out for your rights.

If you are having trouble with the estate, the insurance or any part of the "death duties" forced on you, say what you need. Ask and ask until you find someone who will help you - your attorney, an accountant, a good friend. There will be times when you will be overwhelmed.

Remember:

You are the consumer.

You have a right to be heard.

♦Having feelings.

You will feel deeply. As Jean's poem says, it feels like forever. Grief feels as if it will never end. You have waves of sadness, anger, depression and extreme loneliness. You have a right to feel these emotions and a right to express them safely in ways that do not harm you or anyone else. You have the right to cry in public and in private, to yell in the shower and to hammer a pillow with your fists. You have a right to be a little different right now.

♦Talking out your grief.

You have a right to share your feelings in a safe place. Find someone who will listen and/or a support group.

> **Forever**
>
> Grief
>
> feels
>
> like
>
> f-o-r-e-v-e-r
>
> and
>
> that's
>
> a
>
> very
>
> long
>
> time.
>
> *Jean McGrew*

♦ Setting the limits you need

There will be times when you don't want to see people. There will be times when you need to be alone, to take a day off, to collect yourself. You have a right to tell people, even your family, to give you some space and some time.

Taking care of yourself means so many things. It means being strong when someone needs to lean on you, but finding someone upon whom you can lean, too. You are bent and broken right now. An old grief saying goes, "You can't lean on a tree that is already bending." There may be times when you need to tell those closest to you that they need to find someone else to lean on for awhile.

When you can understand each other, you are like the old story of the dying grandfather who gave each family member one stick and asked them to break the sticks. After a little effort, each stick was broken. Then he gave them three sticks bound together and asked them to break the bundle. No matter how hard each tried, the sticks that were together would not break.

You can expect some discord in your family after death. Anger and disruption seem to follow death like a hungry cat follows a fat mouse. You may feel as if you are indeed a bundle of sticks and everyone is trying to break you.

My mom and aunt had this really big fight after Grandma died. They had never fought like that before. It scared me. It was a long time before they talked to each other again.

If you recognize that everyone has strong feelings and is vulnerable now it may help you keep some perspective. This is definitely a time to avoid grudges and to express your anger in a healthy way.

Keep your sticks bundled together if you possibly can. Give everyone some space and understanding.

Your Body Grieves, Too

You are stressed! The emotions that hit you and come from you when you grieve are, without a doubt, some of the most stressful feelings you've ever had.

Just as your heart aches and your soul begins to heal, your body is likely to ache and need to heal, too. You may:
be tremendously tired
hungry all the time
never hungry
sigh often and long (to get air into your lungs)
forget things
not be able to concentrate
be confused
jump at the slightest noise
have vague aches and pains, sometimes the same ones your loved one had before death.
You may want to sleep all the time.
You may not be able to sleep at all.

> *Grief*
> *climbs in bed*
> *with me,*
> *its ice cold feet*
> *wearing*
> *HIS socks.*

You may not care how you look now, either.
While it's appropriate and healthy to spend some time wearing nothing but a bathrobe and comfy slippers, there's going to be a time when you have to take off your grief clothes and start to live again.

In her book, *Women Who Run With The Wolves,* Clarissa Pinkola Estes talks about the life/death/life cycle.
You've had life with your loved one.
You've experienced Lady Death.
Now you have a new life to face and hopefully, learn to love and enjoy.

Be good to your body. You deserve to live. You may feel miserable, but the pain will slowly get better. There are some things you can do to help it along.

Eat right. Fuel your body with the best there is.

Drink water. Pour 8 glasses into a pitcher and drink it during the day.

Sleep. Catch a nap during the day if you need to.

Exercise. Put your grief in your pocket and take it for a walk. If you've never exercised, start slowly. Once you move your body you move your emotions, too.

Kelly Osmont in *More Than Surviving* says:

"I made a vow. The way I grieved needed to be a tribute to my son, who wasn't a quitter. I remembered days when he talked himself out of excuses for running when he didn't feel like it. I remembered how hard he fought after each surgery. I remembered how much he would have loved to stay alive. So as each excuse surfaced, I imagined a windshield wiper in front of me, swishing it away. Then I would just go do it."

Be with people. Once you get out you're likely to laugh. Give yourself a treat now and then.

I hung a sign in my kitchen that says:
The Four Basic Food Groups:
Chocolate Fudge
Chocolate Brownies
Chocolate Cake
Diet Pop.

Above all, know that **you are not alone.** There are people to help and support you. As you start this new life cycle, you'll face a journey.

It's not a journey you have to travel alone.

Your Authors:

In 1978, Joy and Dr. Marvin Johnson founded Centering Corporation. Since then, Centering has become a well-respected, worldwide grief resource center. The Johnsons live in Omaha, Nebraska and have 6 children and 7 grandchildren.

The title and artwork is from an earlier book by Ed Vining, funeral director, Stephen Minister and loving friend. The pages on children and teens were done by Janet Sieff, Centering Corporation.

Other Books You May Find Helpful

For Widows:
Companion Through The Darkness
Widow
Does Anybody Else Hurt This Bad and Live?

For Widowers:
Cowbells and Courage
A Look In The Mirror
Men and Grief

For Parents:
Dear Parents
Goodbye My Child
Children Die, Too
How Do We Tell The Children?
Thank You For Coming To Say Goodbye
The Grieving Child

For Children:
Where's Jess?
How It Feels When A Parent Dies
For Those Who Live

All of the above books are available from: Centering Corporation
1531 N. Saddle Creek Rd, Omaha NE 68104
Phone: 402-553-1200   Fax: 402-553-0507